Introduction

Discover the joys of cooking! With this book, not only will you learn how to prepare easy and delicious dishes, but you will also journey around the world tasting new dishes from many countries. In this way, you will meet other children who eat different foods and who have different customs than you do.

Children introduce each recipe, and you can find out where their countries are on the map of the world shown on the inside cover of the book. Each recipe has a number, which is also the number of the country on the map. For example, the recipe from Belgium is number one; can you find Belgium on the map? (Hint: just find number one and you have found Belgium!). So, as you prepare each recipe, learn more about the children in the matching country by asking yourself, or any adult, about their customs and everyday life.

Before you begin cooking, carefully read the **15 Practical Pieces of Advice** on cooking that are given at the beginning of this book. Also read the **Cooking Hints**; they'll make your cooking venture much easier! Each delicious dish will be enough to serve four persons.

If you turn to the middle of the book, you will find some **Hints for Healthy Eating** and you can also discover how the United Nations Children's Fund is helping children in other parts of the world who are not as fortunate as you.

Acknowledgements

UNICEF wishes to thank everyone who contributed to this book.

15 Practical Pieces of Advice

1 First, wash your hands well before preparing a dish and put on an apron!

2 Read the recipe right through before you make anything.

3 Arrange all the ingredients and utensils you will need in front of you.

4 Don't forget a damp sponge in case you spill something.

5 If you have to cut something, use a cutting board and a good knife.

6 Use your knife with care.

7 If you use a pan, turn the handle to the side away from the heat to avoid knocking it over accidentally.

8 Use large, stable bowls on a table to mix ingredients.

9 If you need the oven, ask for help to turn it on a quarter of an hour before needing to use it.

10 Hold hot dishes with oven mitts or pot holders and always put them on a trivet.

11 Turn off the oven or the burner as soon as your dish is cooked.

12 Arrange your dish nicely – presentation is very important.

13 Then wash all the utensils and tidy up.

14 Throw away all the packages and refuse.

15 Whatever recipe you choose, ask an adult to help you to avoid any possible mishaps!

And now, let's start work and have fun!

Cooking Hints

To separate egg whites from yolks:
   Put 2 bowls in front of you, one for the whites, the other for the yolks. Crack the egg shell against the side of the bowl for the whites – open the egg with both thumbs and drop the white into one bowl, passing the yolk from one half of the shell into the other.

To stiffen egg whites:
   Put the whites in a bowl and let come to room temperature; when starting to beat them with an electric beater, add a pinch of salt.

To make cake batter:
   Take the butter out of the refrigerator at least 1 hour ahead so that it is soft.

To grease a cake pan:
   Put some butter on a piece of bread and rub it on the bottom and sides of your pan.

To sift flour:
   Pass the flour through a large, fine sieve to get rid of the lumps.

To grate lemon rind:
Wash and wipe the lemon and grate the peel against the fine side of the grater.

To peel an onion:
Peel it under running water and cut it on a damp board, then you will not cry.

To peel tomatoes:
Put tomatoes in a bowl. Pour boiling water over them. Leave for 1 minute. Pour out water and hold tomatoes under running cold water; the skin will peel off easily.

To chop herbs and parsley:
Cut off the stalks, put the leaves in a narrow glass. Cut them in the glass with scissors.

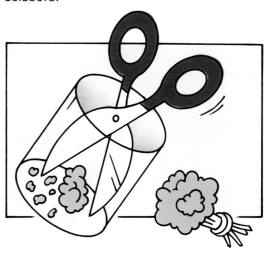

To thicken sauce:
Always mix the flour with twice as much cold milk before adding it to the other ingredients. This will prevent the sauce from getting lumpy.

BELGIUM
Royal Salad

2 1/2 cups string beans

3 heads of chicory lettuce

3 apples

3 medium potatoes

100 g chopped lettuce

4 tablespoons oil

2 tablespoons vinegar

Salt and pepper

M Wash the potatoes

Boil the potatoes in salted water, until tender

Drain, peel and slice them

1

Wash and dice the apples

Wash the chicory, slice the inner leaves

Set aside nice outer leaves

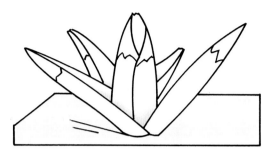

Break off the lettuce leaves, wash them and cut them into strips

Rinse the beans and drain

Put the vinegar and a little salt and pepper in a bowl, slowly add the oil, whisking constantly

Combine the apples, potatoes and chicory. Add the dressing

Line a bowl with the whole chicory leaves, pile the vegetables in the middle and decorate with the lettuce leaves

Shrimp with orange

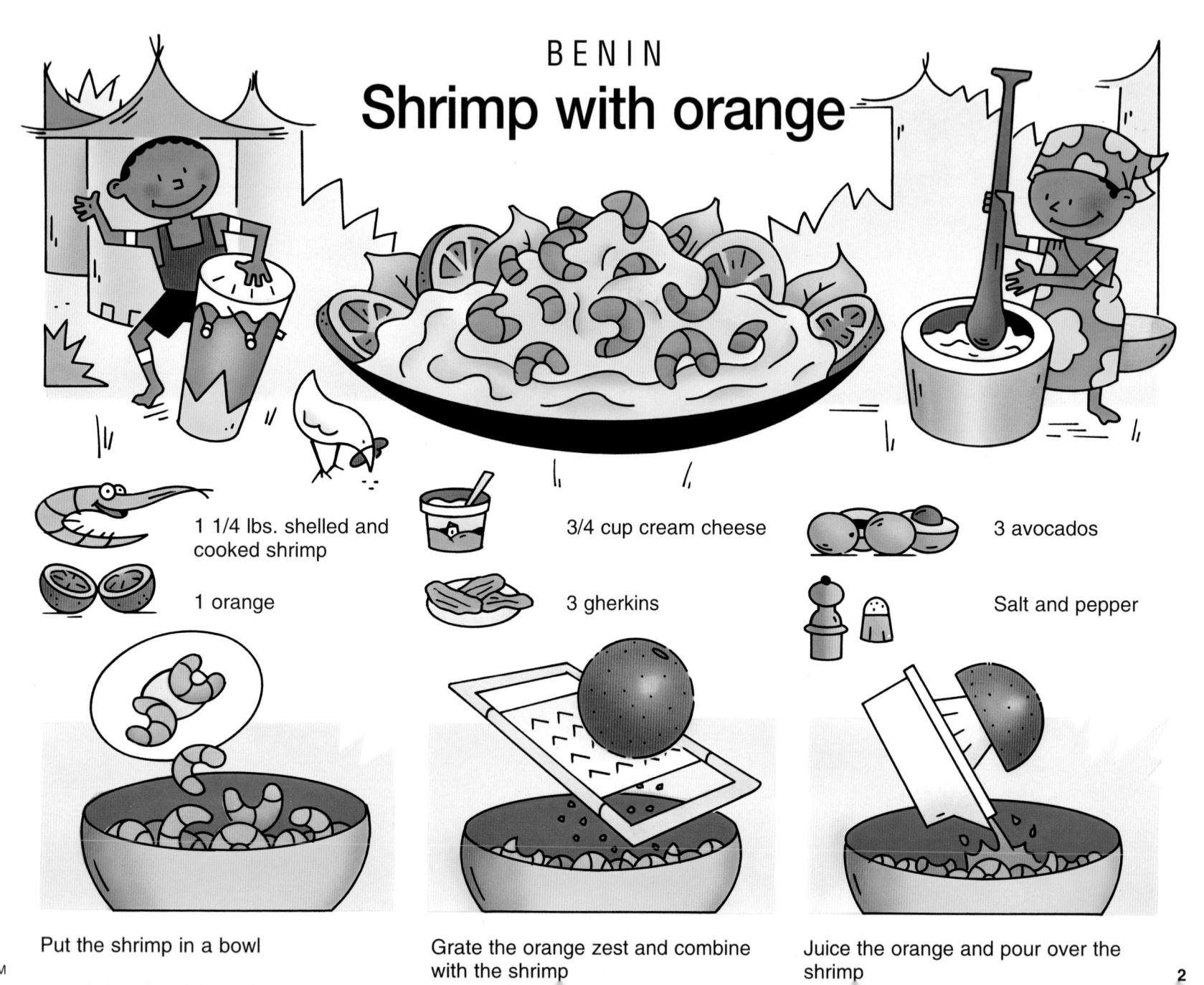

1 1/4 lbs. shelled and cooked shrimp

3/4 cup cream cheese

3 avocados

1 orange

3 gherkins

Salt and pepper

Put the shrimp in a bowl

Grate the orange zest and combine with the shrimp

Juice the orange and pour over the shrimp

M

2

Mash the cream cheese

Season with salt and pepper

Add the cream cheese to the shrimp, combine well

Cut the avocados in half and remove the pit

Remove the flesh of the avocado with a spoon

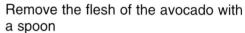

Put the avocado and gherkins into a blender and blend until there are no lumps

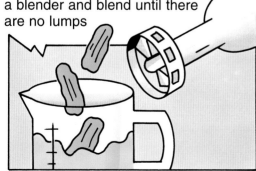

Serve the shrimp on the avocado sauce

Guacamole

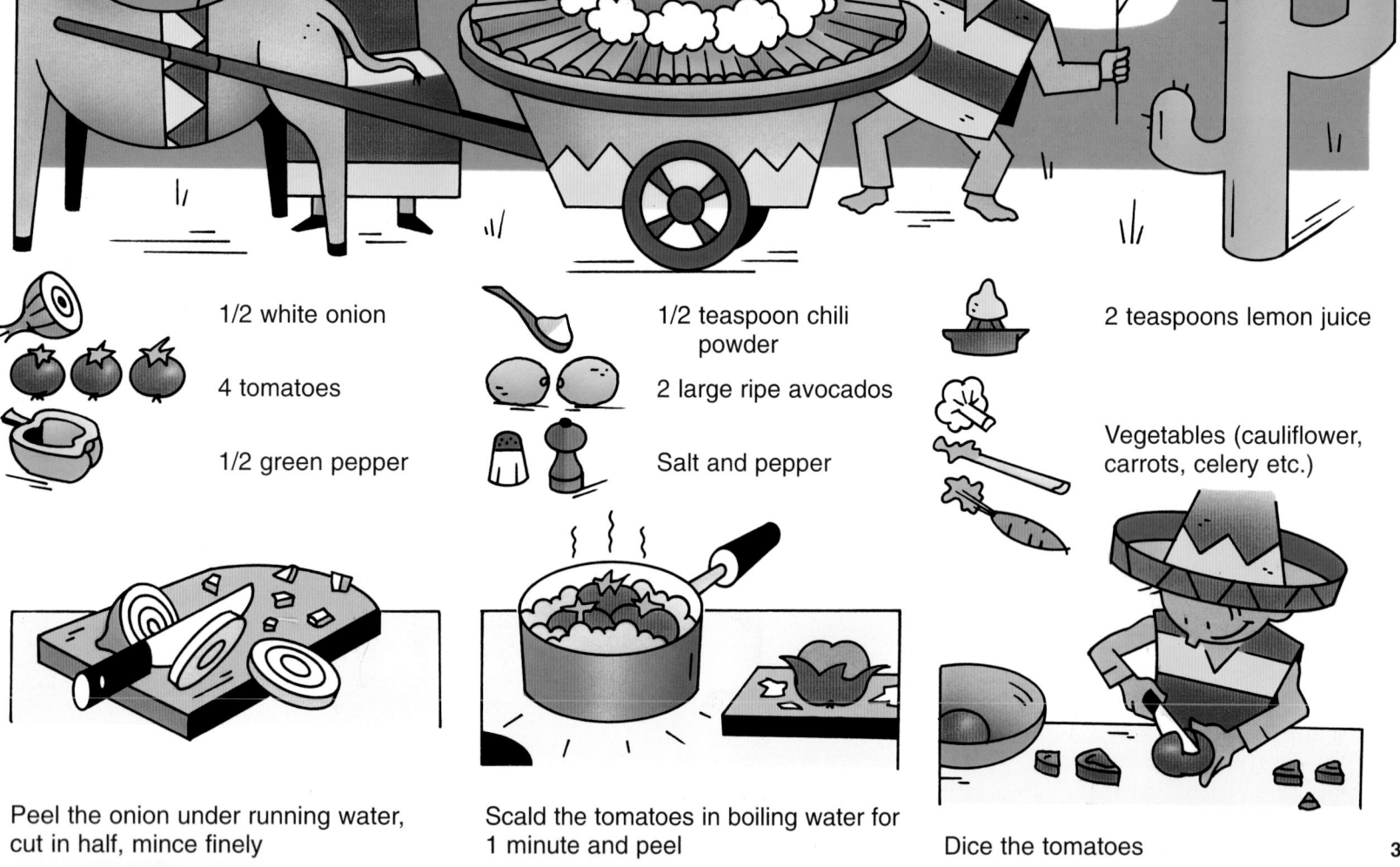

1/2 white onion

4 tomatoes

1/2 green pepper

1/2 teaspoon chili powder

2 large ripe avocados

Salt and pepper

2 teaspoons lemon juice

Vegetables (cauliflower, carrots, celery etc.)

Peel the onion under running water, cut in half, mince finely

Scald the tomatoes in boiling water for 1 minute and peel

Dice the tomatoes

Remove the seeds from the pepper and dice half

Cut the avocados in half and remove the pit

Scoop out the flesh with a spoon and mash it

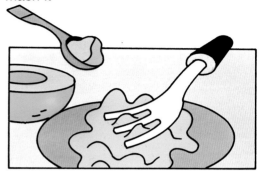

Put all ingredients into a bowl and mix

Add the lemon juice, salt and pepper and a pinch of chili

Mix well

Peel and cut the vegetables

Put the guacamole in a bowl in the middle of a large platter of vegetables

Caesar Salad

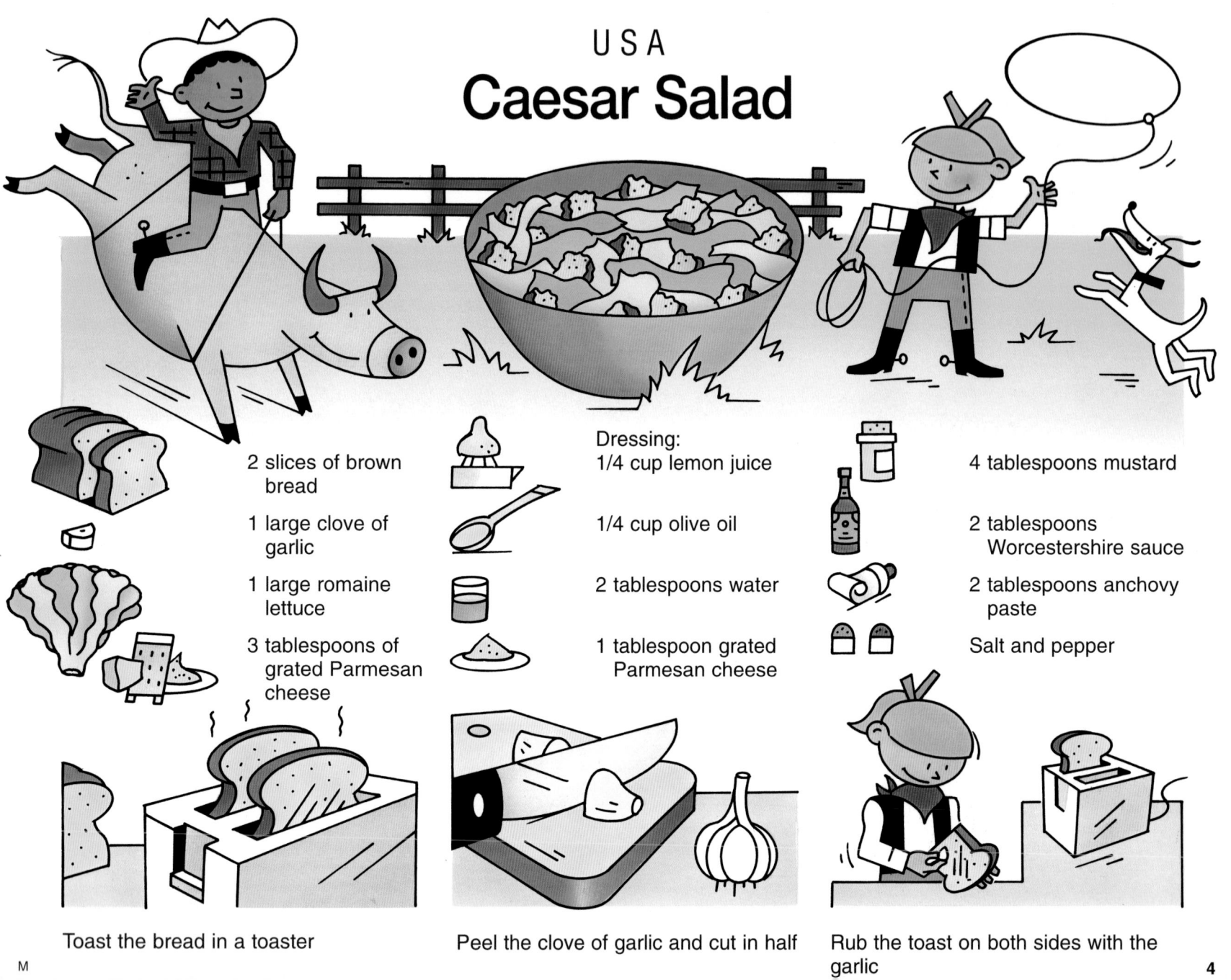

2 slices of brown bread

1 large clove of garlic

1 large romaine lettuce

3 tablespoons of grated Parmesan cheese

Dressing:
1/4 cup lemon juice

1/4 cup olive oil

2 tablespoons water

1 tablespoon grated Parmesan cheese

4 tablespoons mustard

2 tablespoons Worcestershire sauce

2 tablespoons anchovy paste

Salt and pepper

Toast the bread in a toaster

Peel the clove of garlic and cut in half

Rub the toast on both sides with the garlic

Cut the toast into cubes to make croutons

Mince the garlic finely

Mix the lemon juice, garlic, water and oil

Add the mustard, Worcestershire sauce and anchovy paste

Mix well, salt and pepper to taste

Wash the lettuce and dry well

Cut the lettuce into strips

Add the dressing and toss gently

Add the Parmesan and croutons and serve

Hanna's Salad

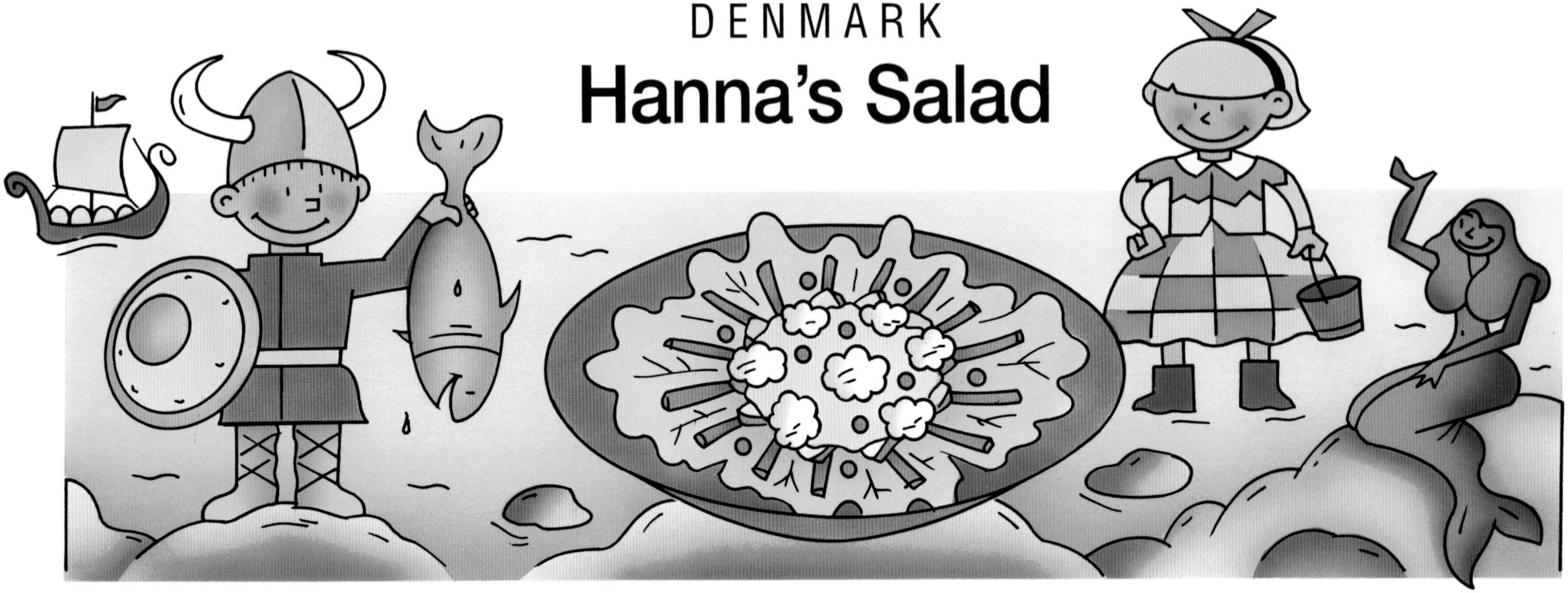

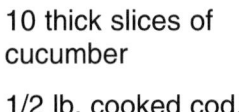

 4 lettuce leaves

 10 thick slices of cucumber

3 teaspoons lemon juice

2 carrots

1/2 lb. cooked cod, skinned and boned

1/2 teaspoon salt

1/2 cup peas

2/3 cup sour or heavy cream

1 teaspoon curry powder

Wash and dry the lettuce leaves

Peel the carrots and slice thinly

Cut the slices of cucumber into small cubes

Cook the peas in salted water and chill them

Mix the cream, lemon juice, salt and curry powder

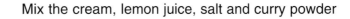

Flake the fish using 2 forks

Take four plates and place a lettuce leaf on each. Put a little carrot and cucumber in the middle of each plate

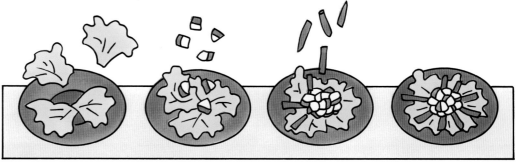

Put the fish on top

Pour the dressing over the salad

Decorate with the peas

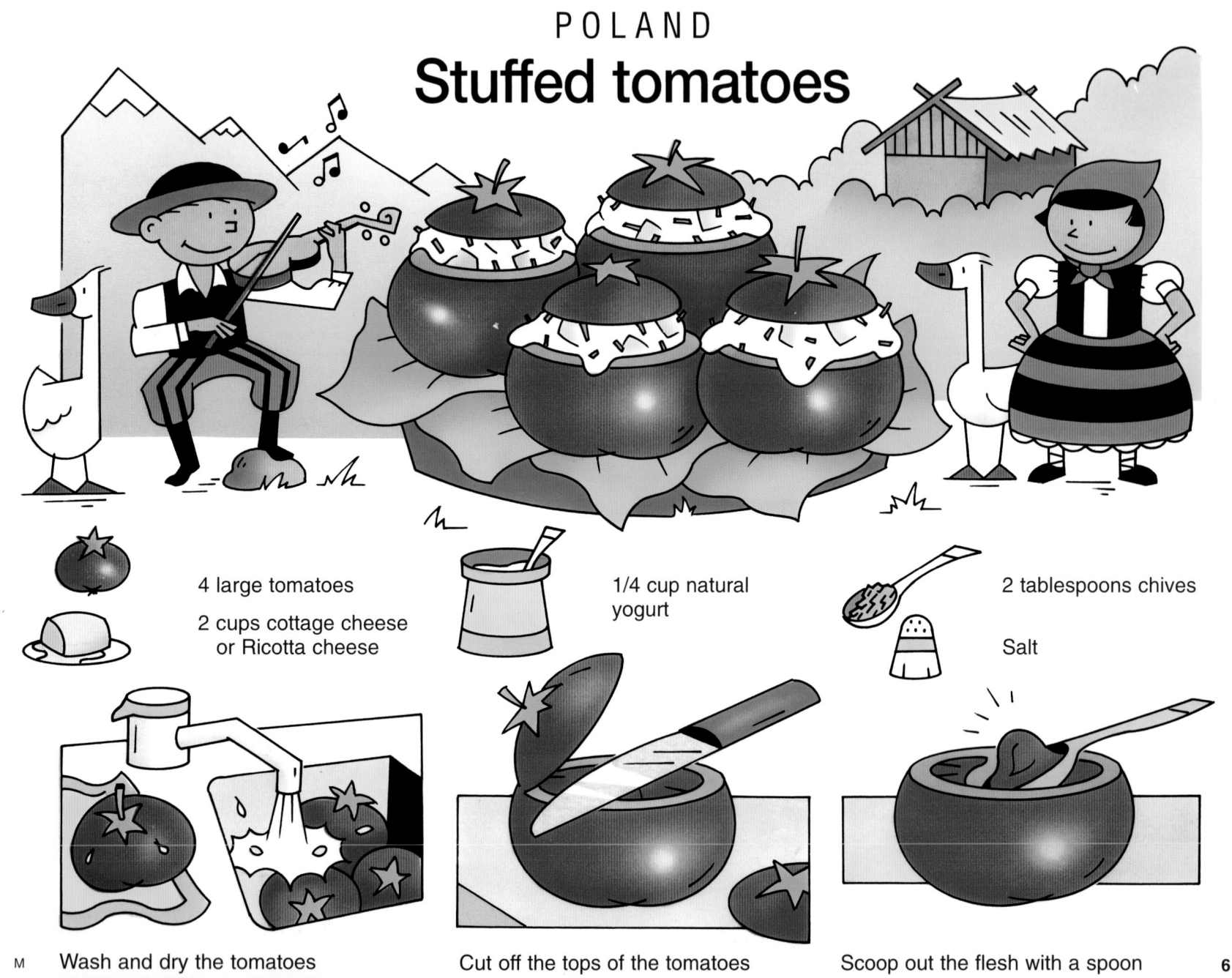

POLAND
Stuffed tomatoes

4 large tomatoes

2 cups cottage cheese or Ricotta cheese

1/4 cup natural yogurt

2 tablespoons chives

Salt

Wash and dry the tomatoes

Cut off the tops of the tomatoes

Scoop out the flesh with a spoon

Sprinkle a little salt inside the tomato and turn upside down to drain

Rinse the chives and cut into 1/2" pieces

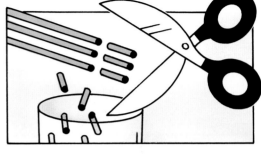

Dice the cheese if using Ricotta

Add the yogurt, chives and a little salt

Mix carefully until uniform consistency

Fill the tomatoes with the mixture

Put the top back on each tomato

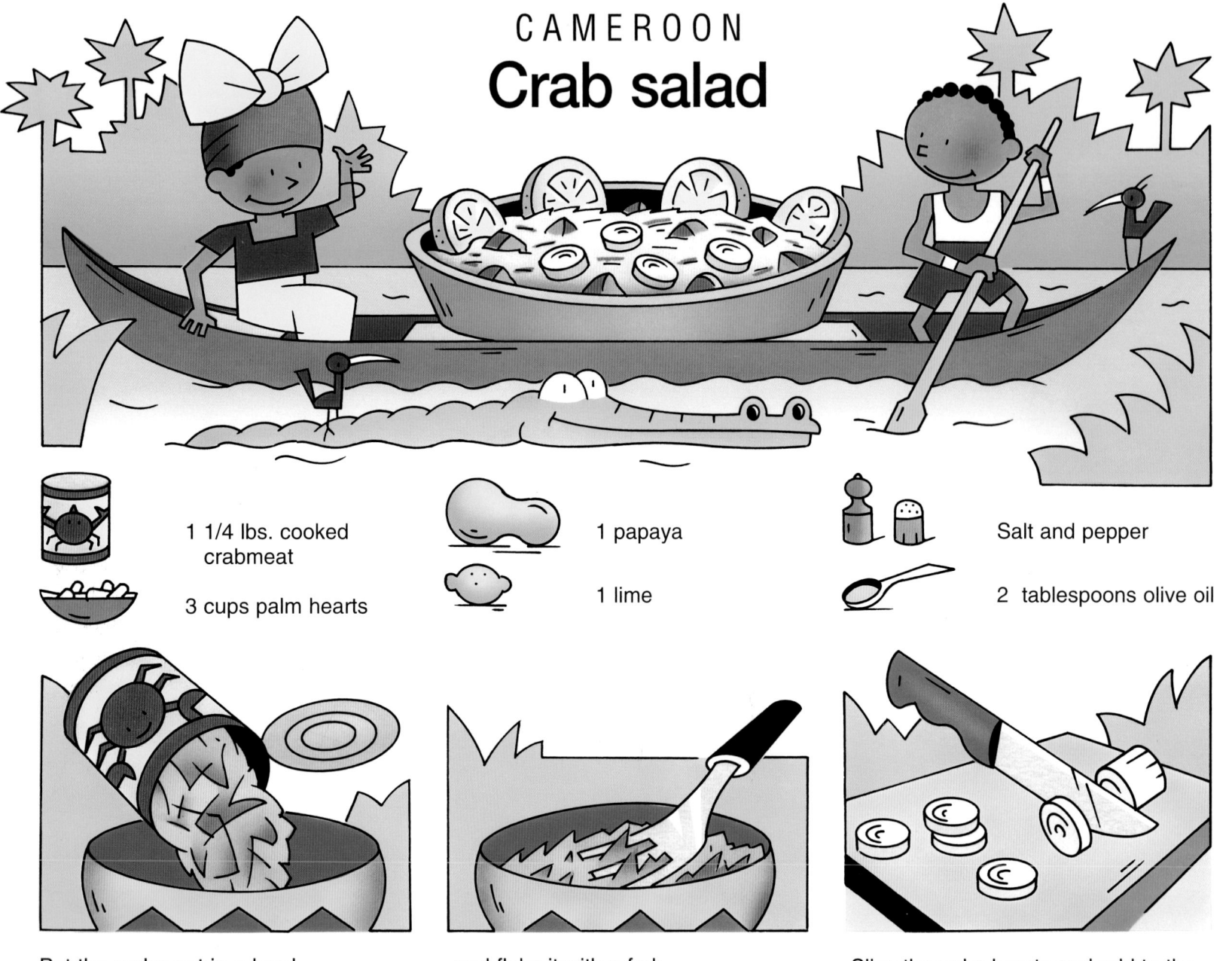

CAMEROON
Crab salad

1 1/4 lbs. cooked crabmeat

3 cups palm hearts

1 papaya

1 lime

Salt and pepper

2 tablespoons olive oil

Put the crabmeat in a bowl

and flake it with a fork

Slice the palm hearts and add to the crabmeat

Peel the papaya and remove the pit

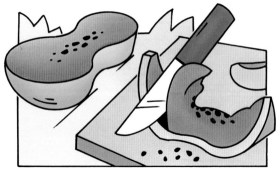

Dice and add to the crabmeat mixture

Squeeze the lime and pour the juice over the mixture

Season with salt and pepper

Add the oil

Mix well

Leave in the refrigerator for one hour before serving

GREECE
Grilled pepper salad

6 green peppers

6 red peppers

Salt and pepper

Oil

Vinegar

Light the grill

Wash the peppers

Remove the stalk and cut in half

Remove the seeds

Arrange on a baking sheet (open side down)

Put under the grill

Grill for 2 minutes

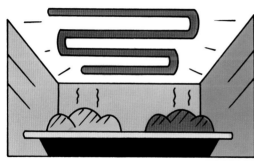

Plunge the peppers into cold salted water

Skin them

Cut them into strips of about 3/4" width

Arrange them on a plate and sprinkle with a little oil and vinegar, salt and pepper

SPAIN
Paella

2 cups rice

3 chicken breasts

3/4 lb. shelled shrimp

3/4 cup peas

1 small can sweet red peppers

1/2 onion

1 clove garlic, crushed

1 small tomato

4 cups water

2/3 cup oil

Salt and pepper

1/2 cup parsley

Chop the parsley

Heat the oil in a large frying-pan

Sauté the chicken breasts until golden

M

Remove to a plate and keep warm

Quarter the onion and the tomato and fry them

Add the rice and stir for 1 minute

Add the chicken

Add the water and bring to a boil

Add the shrimp, garlic, parsley, peas and red peppers

Cook until all the water has been absorbed

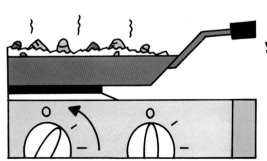

Turn the heat off and allow to stand for a further 10 minutes before serving

Baked potatoes

4 large potatoes

1/4 cup chives

1 cup sour cream

Pre-heat the oven to 400°

Scrub the potatoes under running water

Pour a little oil into the palm of your hands

Rub the potatoes in your hands and prick them with a fork

Wrap each potato in aluminium foil

Put the potatoes on a baking sheet and place in the oven

Bake for 60 minutes

Wash and chop the chives

Pour the cream into a bowl, add the chives and mix

Take the potatoes out and remove the foil

Make two wide slits in each potato in the shape of a cross

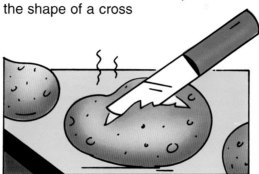

Pour the cream into the slits.

INDIA
Beef curry

2 cups stewing steak

Salt and pepper

2 medium onions

1 clove of garlic

2 tablespoons curry powder

1 tablespoon flour

2 cups beef stock

1 tablespoon mango chutney

1 tablespoon brown sugar

Juice of half a lemon

2 tablespoons butter

Pre-heat the oven to 350°

Peel the onions and garlic and slice finely

Heat the butter in a saucepan

M

Fry the onions and garlic gently in the butter

Add the curry powder and stir well for 5 minutes

Add the flour and stock

Boil, stirring continuously

Add the mango chutney, brown sugar, lemon juice and a little salt and pepper

Cut the steak into 1 inch cubes and put them in a casserole dish

Pour the sauce onto the meat

Cover the dish

Cook in the oven for about 1 1/2 hours

Rice with cod

2 cups of rice

4 cups of water

1 large onion

1 large cod fillet

1 clove garlic

1 carrot

1 slice of smoked bacon (1/4" thick)

1 bunch of parsley

2 tablespoons olive oil

M Rinse the fish under running water

Cut it into 1" cubes

Cut the bacon into small pieces

12

Peel the carrot, onion and garlic

Cut them into thin slices

Heat the oil in a wide saucepan

Fry the vegetables gently in the oil

Add the bacon and rice and fry gently

Cover with water. Cook over medium heat for 15 minutes

Put the fish on top of the rice mixture, let stand covered

When the water has been absorbed, the rice is cooked. Rinse the parsley and chop. Decorate the dish with the parsley

ITALY
Macaroni with bacon

2 1/2 cups macaroni

1 onion

1 red pepper

1/2 cup bacon

2 cups tomato sauce

1 cup heavy cream

2 tablespoons olive oil

Peel the onion under running water

Slice thinly

Cut the pepper in half and remove the seeds. Cut into strips

Fry the onion and the pepper in 2 tablespoons of oil

Cut the bacon into thin strips, add to the onion and pepper

Remove the pepper when it has changed colour

Add the tomato sauce and let simmer for 15 minutes

Bring 2 quarts of salted water to a boil in a large saucepan

Add the macaroni, cook until tender

Remove the sauce from the stove and add the pepper.

Add the cream and mix well

Drain the macaroni, pour the sauce over and mix gently

Chicken with preserved lemons

2 lbs. chicken (cut into pieces)

3 onions

1 bunch cilantro

Pinch of saffron

Salt and pepper

4 small lemons in brine

1 teaspoon ginger

3-4 tablespoons oil

Peel the onions and slice finely

Heat a little oil in a heavy saucepan

Add the onions and chicken pieces

Fry until golden

Add a little salt, pepper, the ginger and the saffron

Cover with water and add the bunch of cilantro

Let simmer over a low heat for 40 minutes

Take the chicken out and keep it warm

Cut the lemons into quarters and remove the peel

Add the peel to the chicken sauce and simmer for a further 5 minutes

Homemade hamburgers

2 lbs. lean ground beef

1 egg, beaten

1/4 cup fresh breadcrumbs

1 onion

1/4 cup tomato Ketchup

1 tablespoon oregano

4 hamburger buns

4 thin slices of Swiss cheese

4 slices of tomato

4 lettuce leaves

1/4 cup mustard

Salt and pepper

M Peel the onions under running water

Chop very finely

Add the ground beef and beaten egg

15

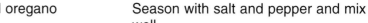

Add the breadcrumbs and mix well

Add the Ketchup and oregano

Season with salt and pepper and mix well

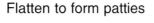

Shape into four balls

Flatten to form patties

Heat 2 tablespoons butter in a large frying-pan

Fry the hamburgers 5 minutes on each side

Cut the buns in half and spread one half with mustard

Place the hamburger on top, then the slice of cheese, add the tomato and lettuce leaf and close the bun

15

Fillets of flounder with mushrooms

1 can mushrooms
(sliced)

4 fillets of flounder

1 cup cream

Butter for the dish

Salt and pepper

Preheat the oven to 400°

Butter an oven-proof dish

Place the fish in it

M

Season with salt and pepper

Open the mushroom can

Rinse the mushrooms under cold water and drain

Spread the mushrooms over the fish

Cover with the cream

Place the baking dish in the center of the oven

Bake 20-25 minutes, or until golden

Hints for Healthy Eating

To function properly, your body needs the energy and the nutrients (proteins, vitamins and minerals) that you find in the foods you eat every day.

Energy

Your body cells, that are at work day and night, need energy. You use up more energy when you take part in any physical activity, such as running, jumping, etc.

Also in cold weather you use more energy to fight against the cold and to make up for the heat your body has lost.

Certain nutrients such as sugars, fats and proteins provide energy.

Nutrients

To build, maintain and strengthen your body, you need many nutrients every day.

There are four necessary food groups :
— Bread and cereals : contain glucides, vitamin B, iron, water and fiber that enable your intestines to function properly.
— Milk and milk products : contain glucides, lipides, proteins, water, vitamin B, and calcium for your bones.
— Fruits and vegetables : contain glucides, fiber, water and vitamins A and C.
— Meat, eggs, fish and legumes : contain lipides, protein, iron, water and vitamin B.

Balance

To properly balance your diet, choose foods from each of the four food groups for every meal (breakfast, lunch and supper) every day, using as many different combinations as possible.

Most importantly, do not forget to start your day with a good breakfast to restore water to your body, and provide it with the energy to help build, maintain and nourish your body cells.

Water

The body is made up of 70 % water. As you can see above, all foods contain water, but because your body continuously loses water, you need to drink at least one quart of it each day, to make up for this loss.

Beware

Be careful of sweets, candy, chocolate, sodas and lemonades. They are low in nutrients, but are full of sugar that spoil your teeth.

Food for all Children: it's their Right!

This book, published by UNICEF, helps you get to know children from other countries on other continents, through their cooking. But do you know what UNICEF is?

Throughout the world, children of your age have the same needs as you do. They need to eat well to become big and strong. They need to go to school to learn so that they will have a job when they are adults. They also need to get proper care when they are ill and, like you do, they need love and affection.

All these needs must be satisfied if all of the children in the world are to grow up in good health and become happy, well-rounded adults. These needs are the rights of all children. For this reason, what is called "The Declaration of the Rights of the Child" was created : it is an official document that includes all these rights, a sort of contract by which all the countries will do every-thing possible to make sure that children's needs will be fully met.

Every country in the world is different. As you know, some countries are a lot poorer than others. In some places, such as Africa, there is a lot of drought which means that sometimes it doesn't rain for years, and the people cannot cultivate the earth to grow their own food. In other parts of the world, floods and cyclones can create great destruction. We often see pictures of these countries on television. Sometimes these countries are also striken by war or disasters such as earthquakes and volcanic eruptions.

This means that many children your age do not live the same way you do and that millions among them do not go to school, are ill, do not receive proper care or do not have enough to eat.

We hope that these millions of children will have a better chance if their rights are really protected, as stated in the "Declaration of the Rights of the Child".

But to come to the aid of all these children in Africa, Asia and Latin America, many years ago, the United Nations Organization created UNICEF which stands for United Nations Children's Fund. UNICEF is present wherever children suffer, and works directly with governments so that children are vaccinated and receive proper care, go to school, have enough food to eat, play and are happy and smiling like you.

TUNISIA
Steamed lamb

1 small shoulder of lamb

1 lb. small waxy potatoes

1/2 tablespoon cumin

Salt and pepper

4 cloves of garlic

Pour a little water into a steamer

Put the lamb in the steamer, close the lid

Cook slowly for 1 hour

M

M

Rinse the potatoes and peel them

Add the potatoes to the steamer

Cook for another 45 minutes

Peel the garlic

Chop finely

Remove the meat and put it on a serving platter

Garnish with the potatoes

Sprinkle the meat and potatoes with the garlic, cumin, salt and pepper

CHINA
Shrimp with tomato

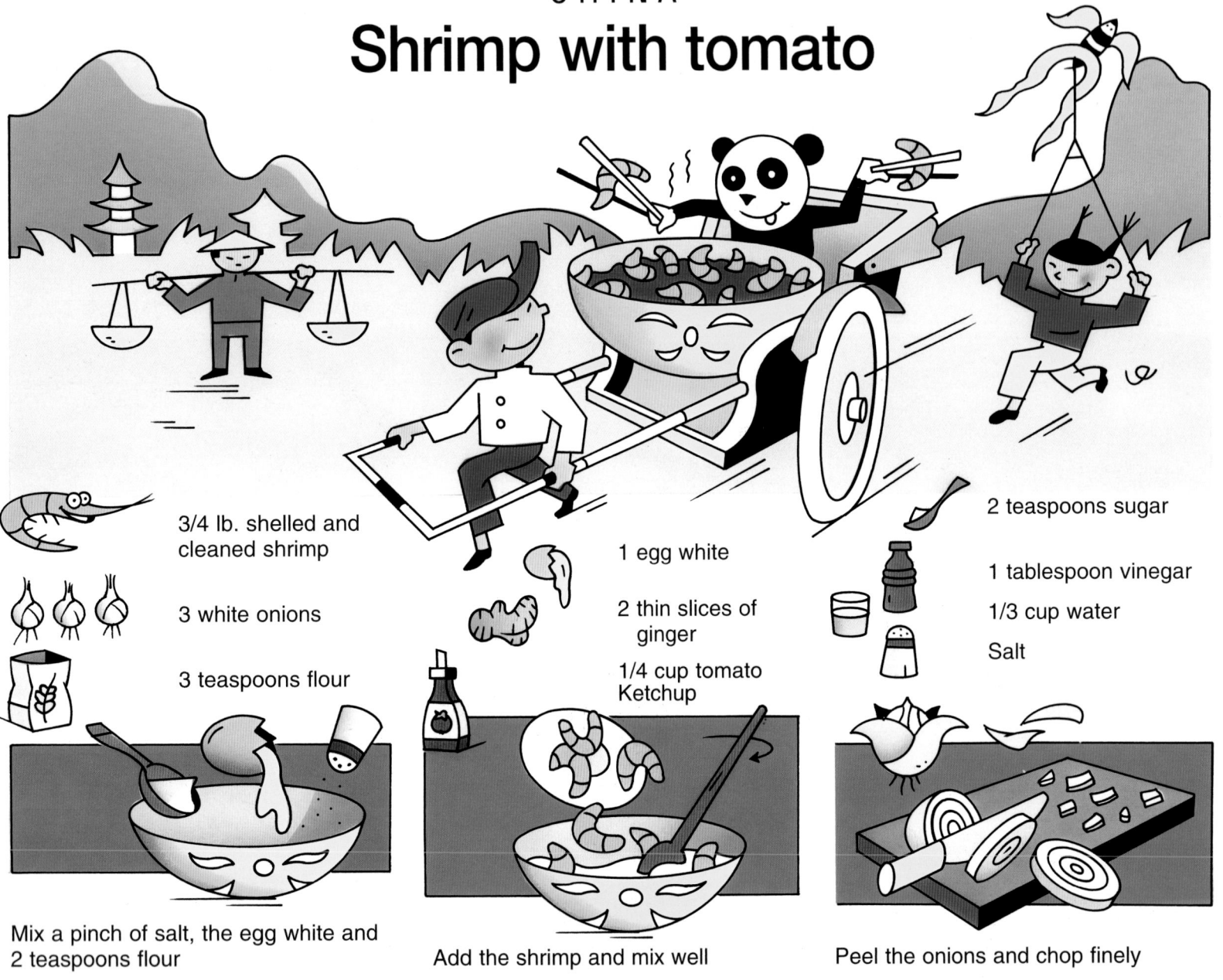

3/4 lb. shelled and cleaned shrimp

3 white onions

3 teaspoons flour

1 egg white

2 thin slices of ginger

1/4 cup tomato Ketchup

2 teaspoons sugar

1 tablespoon vinegar

1/3 cup water

Salt

Mix a pinch of salt, the egg white and 2 teaspoons flour

Add the shrimp and mix well

Peel the onions and chop finely

M

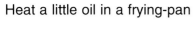

Heat a little oil in a frying-pan

Fry the onions and ginger for 30 seconds

Add the Ketchup, shrimp, sugar and vinegar

Dissolve the rest of the flour in the water

Add

Reduce the heat and let the sauce thicken, stirring continuously. Serve with rice

Caramelized pork

1 1/2 lbs. unsalted pork belly

3 teaspoons brown sugar

1/4 cup soy sauce

2 tablespoons oil

Salt and pepper

M Cut the meat into 2 inch cubes

Put the oil, sugar and soy sauce into a frying-pan

Add the meat and sauté over high heat

19

When the meat has browned, add water to cover the meat by 1 1/2 inches

Simmer over a low heat for 50-55 minutes

Season with salt and pepper

After 40 minutes prick a piece of meat to see if it is cooked

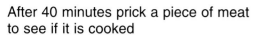

Add a little more water if necessary

Serve with rice

NETHERLANDS
Country omelette

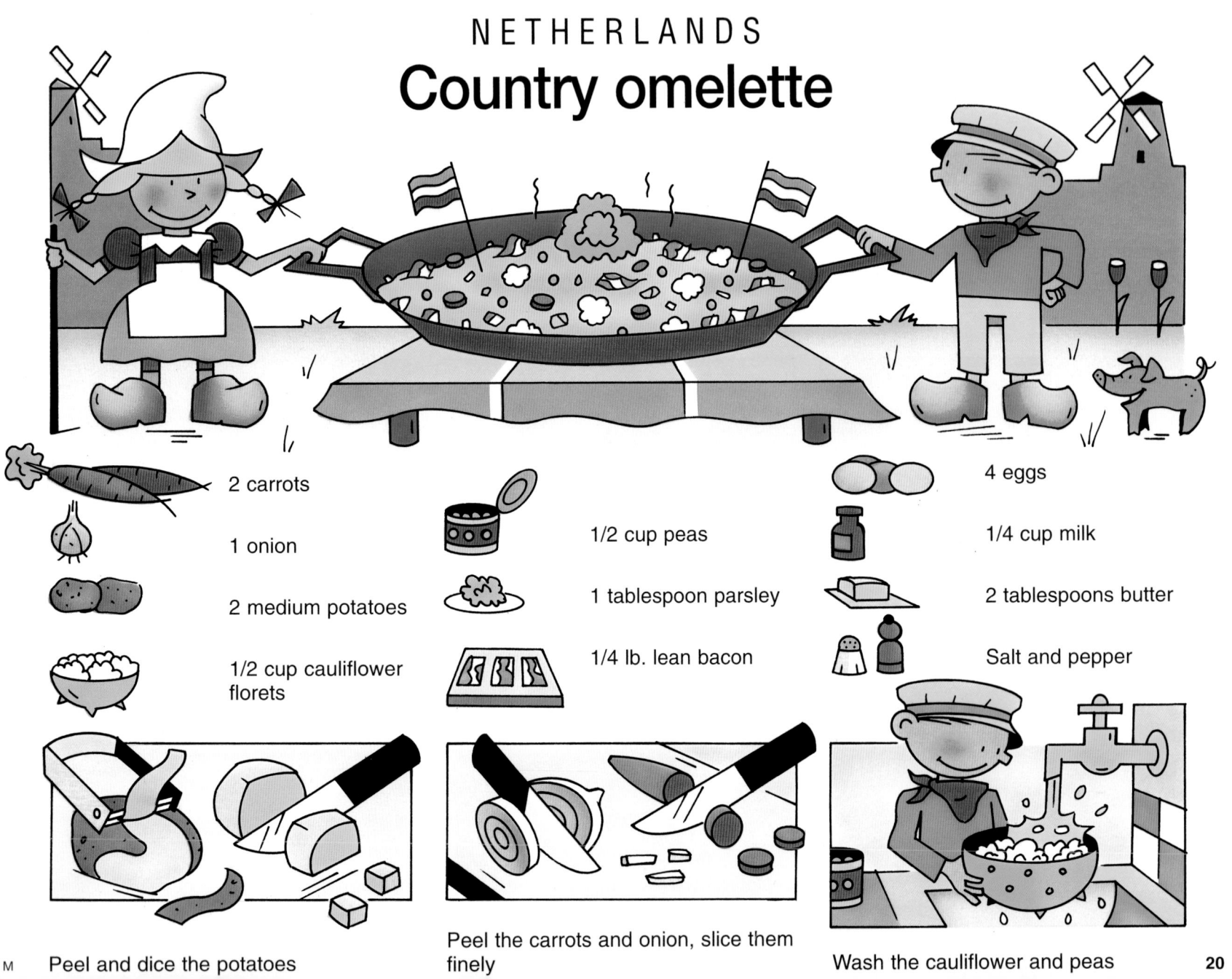

2 carrots

1 onion

2 medium potatoes

1/2 cup cauliflower florets

1/2 cup peas

1 tablespoon parsley

1/4 lb. lean bacon

4 eggs

1/4 cup milk

2 tablespoons butter

Salt and pepper

M Peel and dice the potatoes

Peel the carrots and onion, slice them finely

Wash the cauliflower and peas

Chop the parsley

Melt the butter in a frying-pan

Cut the bacon into thin slices, fry with the onions

Add the vegetables, salt and pepper and cover

Cook over a low heat until the vegetables are cooked

Beat the eggs, milk, and a pinch of salt and pepper

Remove the cover from the frying-pan. Pour the eggs over the vegetables

When the eggs are cooked, lift the edge with a spatula, fold the omelette in half and slide onto a plate

Chicken with cashew nuts

4 chicken breasts

1 egg white

2 tablespoons cornflour/cornstarch

2 tablespoons soy sauce

1 tablespoon sugar

1/2 cup cashew nuts

Salt

M Dice the chicken

Mix the egg white and 1 tablespoon of cornflour

Add a tablespoon of soy sauce and sugar to egg mixture, mix well

Add the diced chicken to the sauce, mix well

Heat a little oil in a frying-pan. Fry the nuts until brown

Pour the nuts onto a plate

Using the same oil, fry the chicken

Remove with a skimmer when golden, set aside

Mix the rest of the cornflour and soy sauce with 1/2 cup water in the frying-pan

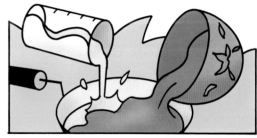

Add the chicken and mix well

Cook for 10 minutes at a medium heat, stirring occasionally

Decorate with the nuts and serve

Hake with chili

4 hake steaks or cod

1/4 cup flour

1/4 cup peanut oil

2 peppers

4 medium tomatoes

1 chili pepper

2 onions

Salt   pepper

M   Wash the fish steaks and pat dry

Put the flour into a shallow bowl

Roll the fish lightly in the flour

Heat the oil and fry the fish until brown

Place the fish on a paper towel to remove excess oil, keep warm

Wash the tomatoes and peppers and remove the seeds

Slice finely, together with the chili pepper and onions

Brown the peppers, chili pepper and onions in the remaining oil

Dice the tomatoes

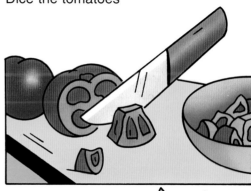

Add to the pepper mixture with a cup of water

Cook for 10 minutes at a high heat, add the fish

Cook for another 5 minutes, and serve

AUSTRIA
Apricot dumplings

1/2 cup water

1/2 cup milk

2/3 cup butter

Pinch of salt

1/4 cup sugar

3/4 cup flour

1 egg

12 fresh apricots

1/2 cup breadcrumbs

Boil the water, milk, 1/4 cup of butter and a little salt

Remove from the stove and add the flour. Mix quickly

Add the egg and continue to mix, until the dough comes away from the sides of the pan

Shape into a loaf and cut into 12 slices

Flatten each slice, remove the pit from the apricot and place an apricot on each slice

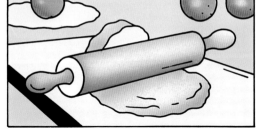

Fold the edges over so that the apricot is completely covered, pinch the seams

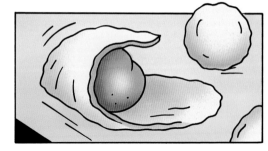

Heat some water in a saucepan

When the water begins to simmer, immerse the first 3 dumplings, cook for 10 minutes

Repeat until all the dumplings are cooked

Melt the remaining butter

Add the breadcrumbs, allow them to toast and add the sugar

Remove from the stove and roll the dumplings in the crumb mixture

UNITED KINGDOM
Apple Crumble

3 lbs. apples

2 tablespoons water

2 tablespoons butter

3/4 cup brown sugar

Pinch of cinnamon

3/4 cup flour

1/3 cup softened butter

3 tablespoons sugar

M Peel and slice the apples thinly

Put them in a saucepan with the water and 2 tablespoons butter

Cover the saucepan and cook over low heat until soft

Remove the saucepan from the stove, mash the apples with a fork

Add the brown sugar and cinnamon, mix well

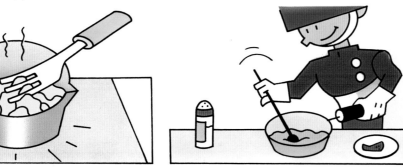

For the pastry, sieve the flour into a large bowl

Add the butter in small pieces and rub in with fingertips

Add the sugar and continue to rub in

Butter an oven-proof dish of 10" diameter

Arrange the apples in the dish. Cover with the pastry

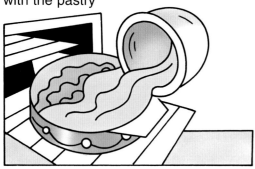

Bake at 400° for 15 minutes. Reduce to 350° and bake for a further 10-15 minutes. Serve warm

HUNGARY
Walnut pancakes

1 1/4 cups flour

1 cup milk

2 tablespoons water

3 eggs

1/2 cup sugar

1/4 cup melted butter

Pinch of salt

1 cup shelled walnuts

1/4 cup fresh cream

3/4 cup bitter chocolate

1/4 cup milk

Butter to cook the pancakes

Mix the flour, 1 cup milk and water in a bowl

Add 1/4 cup sugar, salt, eggs and melted butter, whisk together

Cover the bowl with a clean cloth and let rest 2 hours

Chop the walnuts roughly

Mix them with the rest of the sugar and cream

Melt 1 tablespoon butter in a frying-pan

Pour a ladle of batter into the middle of the frying-pan

When the pancake is cooked on one side, flip it over. Cook the pancake on the other side

Remove and keep warm while cooking the rest

Stuff the pancakes with the walnut cream

Melt the chocolate with 1/4 cup milk

Pour the chocolate sauce over the pancakes

Redcurrant delight

2 cups redcurrants

2 tablespoons sugar

1 1/2 cups milk

1 levelled tablespoon flour

1 teaspoon sugar
1/2 teaspoon vanilla extract

M Wash the redcurrants

Crush them with a fork

Put them into a bowl and sprinkle with a tablespoon of sugar

Dissolve the flour in 2 tablespoons of the milk

Add the sugar and the rest of the milk to the flour mixture

Stir well and pour into a saucepan

Bring slowly to a boil, stirring continuously

Boil for a few minutes, continue stirring

When the sauce is quite thick, add the vanilla and sugar

Allow to cool

When cold, put into the refrigerator for 1 hour

Serve the redcurrants and sauce separately

Chocolate pie

1 cup flour

1/2 cup softened butter

1/4 cup sugar

1 egg yolk

3 tablespoons cream

Pinch of salt

1 1/4 cups fresh cream

1 1/2 cups bitter-sweet chocolate

1 egg yolk

3 tablespoons walnuts

Rub the butter, sugar and salt into the flour with your fingertips

Beat the egg yolk and the 3 tablespoons of cream

Add this mixture gradually to the pastry and form into a ball

Allow to rest 30 minutes

Roll out on a floured surface until big enough to cover the pie dish

Butter the pie dish. Line with the pastry, prick with a fork

Bake at 375° for 10-15 minutes

Heat 1 1/4 cups cream slowly to a boil

Remove the cream from the heat, add the chocolate (in small pieces), stir until melted

Add the egg yolk, mix well

Spread this mixture over the pastry. Decorate your pie with walnuts

Chill until firm

Anis cake

4 eggs

3/4 cup sugar

3 tablespoons water

Rind of 1/2 a lemon

2/3 cup plain flour

Pinch of salt

1 tablespoon anis

Butter for the tin

Preheat your oven to 350°

Separate the egg whites from the yolks

Whisk the yolks with half the sugar

While whisking, add the water slowly

Grate the lemon peel

Add the lemon peel and flour to the mixture

Add the salt and anis

Mix well

Beat the egg whites with the rest of the sugar until stiff

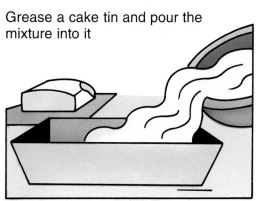

Carefully fold them into the mixture, without mixing very much

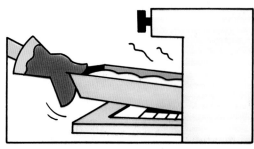

Grease a cake tin and pour the mixture into it

Bake in the middle of the oven for 35-40 minutes

Avocado cream

3 large avocados

2 limes

6 tablespoons sugar

Cut the avocados in half and remove the pit

Scoop out the flesh

Mash to a purée

Cut the limes in half

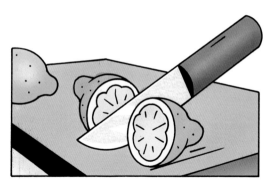

Juice them

Add 1/4 cup juice to the avocado purée

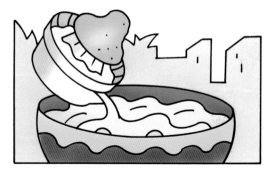

Add 6 tablespoons of sugar and mix well

Serve in individual bowls or in the empty avocado halves

Decorate with a twist of lime

FRANCE
Creme caramel ♪

3 1/4 cups whole milk

6 egg yolks

3 whole eggs

1 cup sugar

1 vanilla bean
(or 1 teaspoon extract)

Brown wrapping paper

Beat the yolks, whole eggs and 1/2 cup sugar

Slowly bring the milk to a boil with the vanilla bean (cut lengthwise)

Remove the vanilla bean

Very slowly add the milk to the eggs, whisking vigorously

Pour the rest of the sugar into a pan with a little water

Heat and stir until the melted sugar turns brown

Pour this caramel into the mould, make sure it spreads evenly

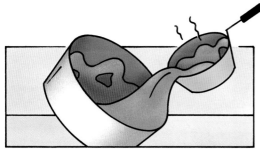

Pour the milk and egg mixture into the mould over the caramel

Fold a sheet of brown paper in half and place on the oven shelf

Fill a baking pan half full with warm water

Place the mould in the water in the baking pan and place it on the paper in the oven. Bake at 300° for 1 1/2 hours

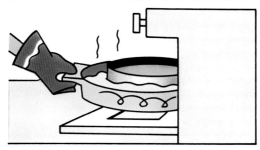

Cool and turn out

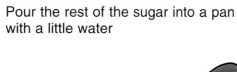

Mango gratin

2 large mangoes

1/3 cup sugar

1 vanilla bean

1/2 cup crushed hazelnuts

1/3 cup butter

3 eggs

Preheat the oven to 400°

Beat half the sugar and one egg vigorously together

Add the crushed hazelnuts and 2 tablespoons melted butter

Mix well, remove the seeds from the vanilla bean and add to the mixture

Peel the mangoes and remove the pit

Purée the flesh of the mangoes in a blender

Add 2 yolks and mix well

Beat 2 egg whites until stiff

Gently fold the whites into the mixture

Pour the mango cream into an oven-proof dish

Cover with the nut cream

Bake for 15 minutes

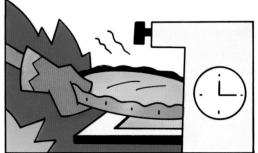

RUSSIA
Pavlova

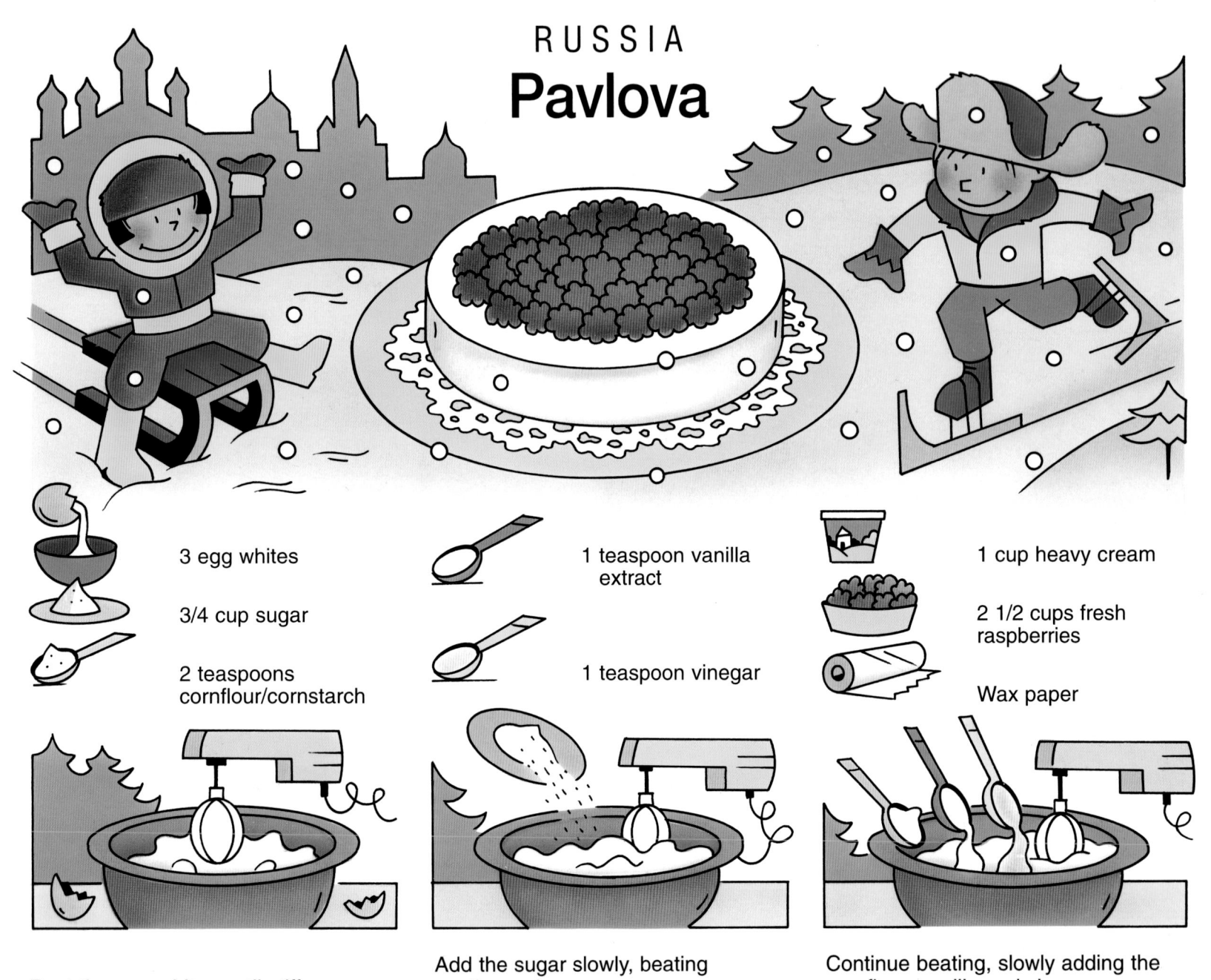

3 egg whites

3/4 cup sugar

2 teaspoons
cornflour/cornstarch

1 teaspoon vanilla
extract

1 teaspoon vinegar

1 cup heavy cream

2 1/2 cups fresh
raspberries

Wax paper

Beat the egg whites until stiff

Add the sugar slowly, beating
continuously

Continue beating, slowly adding the
cornflour, vanilla and vinegar

Cut out a circle of wax paper to cover a cake plate

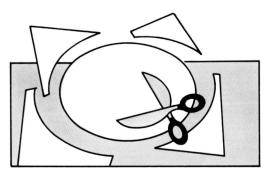

Cover a cake plate

Spread the mixture on the papered cake plate

Bake at 300° for 1 1/2 hours

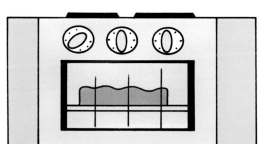

Take out of the oven and remove the paper

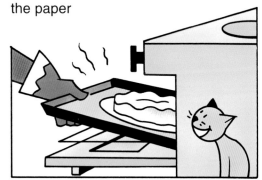

Allow to cool on a cooling rack

Cover with cream and decorate with raspberries

Dessert is served!

ANDORRA :
Comité National d'Andorra per la UNICEF
Avenida del Fener, 14 - Escaldes - Engordany - Andorra - Tél./Fax: (376) 86 71 00

AUSTRALIA :
Australian Committee for UNICEF Limited
P.O. Box N614 - Grosvenor Place
Sydney NSW 2000 - Australia - Tel. : (02) 9290 - 2099 - Fax : (02) 9290 - 2505

BELGIQUE / BELGIË :
Comité belge pour l'UNICEF / Belgisch Comité voor UNICEF
20, avenue des Arts - B - 1040 Bruxelles / 20, Kunstlaan - 1040 Brussel
Tel. : (02) 230 59 70 - Fax : (02) 230 34 62

BRASIL :
Escritorio da UNICEF para cartões de saudacões
Rua México 21, 9° andar - 20031 Rio de Janeiro, RJ, Brasil
Tel. : (021) 240 - 5176 / 220 - 0881 - Fax : (021) 262 - 8324

БЪЛГАРИЯ :
Bulgarian National Committee for UNICEF
18/B Pentcho Slaveikov Blvd. - BG - 1606 Sofia
Tel. : (2) 54 47 30 / 52 14 35 / 51 51 86 - Fax : (2) 80 25 04

CANADA :
Canadian UNICEF Committee / Comité UNICEF Canada
443, Mount Pleasant Road - Toronto, Ontario M4S 2L8 Canada
Tel. : (416) 482 - 4444 - Fax : (416) 482 - 8035

CESKÁ REPUBLICA :
Cesky vybor pro UNICEF
Vyschradska 51 - 12 800 Praha 2 - Czech Republic
Tel. : (2) 244 84551 / 244 84550 - Fax : (2) 249 15328

DANMARK :
Dansk UNICEF Komite
Billedvej 8 - DK - 2100 København Ø - Tel. : 39 29 51 11 - Fax : 39 27 05 77

DEUTSCHLAND :
UNICEF Deutschland
Höninger Weg 104 - D- 50969 Köln - Tel. : 0221 / 936500 - Fax : 0221 / 93650279

EESTI :
UNICEF - I Eesti Rahvuskomitee
Lai 10, P.O. Box 3324 - EE 0001 Tallinn - Eesti
Tel.: (372) 640 6611 - Fax: (372) 649 6612

ESPAÑA :
Comité Español del UNICEF
Mauricio Legendre, 36 - E - 28046 Madrid / Apartado 12021 - E - 28080 Madrid
Tel. : (1) 733 24 15 - Fax : (1) 314 74 75

ΕΛΛΑΔΑ:
Hellenic National Committee for UNICEF
1, Xenias Street - GR - 11527 Athens
Tel. : (01) 748 41 84 - Fax : (01) 778 38 29

FRANCE :
Comité français pour l'UNICEF
3, rue Duguay-Trouin - F - 75282 Paris Cedex 06
Tél. : (1) 44 39 77 77 - Fax : (1) 44 39 77 20

香港 :
Hong Kong Committee for UNICEF
60, Blue Pool Road 3/F - Happy Valley - Hong Kong - Tel. : 2833 - 6139 - Fax : 2834 - 0996

IRELAND :
Irish National Committee for UNICEF
4, St. Andrew Street - IRL - Dublin 2 - Tel. : (01) 677 08 43 / 679 01 22 - Fax : (01) 679 11 52

ישראל:
Israel National Committee for UNICEF
c/o International Cultural Centre for Youth - 12 Emek Rephaim Road - P.O. Box 80 09
93105 Jerusalem - Israel - Tel. : (02) 66 26 19 / 66 41 44 - Fax : (02) 66 66 20

ITALIA :
Comitato italiano per l'UNICEF
Via Vittorio Emanuele Orlando, 83 - I - 00185 Roma
Tel. : (06) 478 091 - Fax : (06) 478 09 270

日本 :
Japan Committee for UNICEF
UNICEF House 31-10, Daikyo-Cho, Shinjuku-ku, Tokyo 160 - Japan
Tel. : (03) 3355 3255 - Fax : (03) 3355 3830

الاردن:
UNICEF MENARO
Comprehensive Commercial Center - Jabal Amman, 3rd Circle - P.O. Box 811721
Amman, Jordan - Tel. : (6) 629571 / 629612 / 629586 - Fax : (6) 640049

대한민국:
Korean Committee for UNICEF
17-1, Changsung - Dong-Congro-Ku - Seoul 110-034
Tel. : (2) 736-7862 / 735-2310 - Fax : (2) 738 8504

KYΠPO :
U.N.D.P. / UNICEF
115 Prodromos Street - Strovolos - P.O. Box 5605 - Nicosia - Cyprus
Tel. : (02) 30 20 56 - Fax : (02) 47 64 13

LATVIJA :
Latvian National Commission for UNICEF
Str. Brivibas , 75 - 1047 Riga - Latvija - Tel. /Fax: (12) 27 17 36

LIETUVIA :
UNICEF Lietuvos Nacionalinis Komitetas / Lithuanian Committee for UNICEF
Roziu aleja 4a - 2600 Vilnius - Lietuvia - Tel. : (822) 227 707 - Fax : (822) 227 717

LUXEMBOURG :
Comité luxembourgeois pour l'UNICEF, a.s.b.l.
99, route d'Arlon - L - 1140 Luxembourg - Tél. : (2) 44 87 15 - Fax : (2) 45 53 14

MAGYARORSZÁG :
Az ENSZ Gyermekalap Magyar Nemzeti Bizottsága
Varsányi Iren u. 26.34 - II. Lh. VI. 1.- H - 1027 Budapest
Tel. : 201 49 23 / 155 50 10 - Fax : 155 50 19

NEDERLAND :
Stichting Nederlands Comité UNICEF
St. Barbaraweg 4 - NL - 2516 BT Den Haag / P.O. Box 30603
NL-2500 GP Den Haag - Tel. : (070) 3339333 - Fax : (070) 3824774

NEW ZEALAND :
New Zealand Committee for UNICEF
Room 534, 5th Floor, Harbour City Tower - 29 Brandon Street - Wellington
New Zealand - Tel. : (4) 473 - 0879 / 384 - 8752 - Fax : (4) 499-1308

NORGE :
UNICEF-komiteèn i Norge
Møllergaten 24 N - 0179 Oslo 1
Tel. : 22 36 33 40 - Fax : 22 36 30 10

ÖSTERREICH :
Österreichisches Komitee für UNICEF
Vienna International Centre - U. N. O. City - Wagramer Straße 22
A-1400 Wien - Tel. : (01) 23 60 1556-59 - Fax : (01) 23 98 20

POLSKA :
Polski Komitet UNICEF
Ul. Siennicka 48 - PL - 03-494 Warszawa
Tel. : (022) 13 26 25 - Fax : (022) 10 68 67

PORTUGAL :
Comité Português para a UNICEF
Av. António Augusto de Aguiar, 56 - 3° Esq. - P - 1050 Lisboa
Tel. : (01) 315 29 04 / 315 28 77 - Fax : (01) 54 79 13

REPUBLIKÁ SLOVENIJA :
Slovenski Odbor za UNICEF / Slovenian Committee for UNICEF
Liniiartova 13 - 61000 Ljubljana - Republiká Slovenija
Tel. : (61) 131 43 40 - Fax : (61) 131 43 02

ROMÂNIA :
Comitetul National Român UNICEF
Strada Stirbei Vodă, Nr. 37 - Sectorul 1, Bucuresti - 70732 Bucharest - România
Tel. : (1) 615 76 27 / 311 33 57 - Fax : (1) 312 31 57

SAN MARINO :
Commissione Nazionale Sammarinese per l'UNICEF
c/o Segreteria di Stato per gli Affari Esteri - Palazzo Begni - 47031 San Marino
Tel. : 88 22 26 - Fax : 99 20 18

SCHWEIZ / SUISSE / SVIZZERA :
Schweizerisches Komitee für UNICEF / Comité suisse pour l'UNICEF /
Comitato Svizzero per l'UNICEF
Baumackerstrasse 24 - CH - 8050 Zürich
Tel. : (01) 317 22 66 - Fax : (01) 312 22 76

SLOVENSKÁ REPUBLIKA :
Slovensky vybor pre UNICEF / Slovak Committee for UNICEF
Grosslingova 6 - 811 09 Bratislava - Slovenská Republika
Tel. : (07) 365 082 / 361 948 - Fax : (07) 365 084

SUOMI / FINLAND :
Suomen UNICEF-yhdistys r.y. / Finlands UNICEF -Förening r.f.
Perttulantie 6 - FIN - 00211 Helsinki / Bertasvägen 6 - FIN - 00211 Helsingfors
Tel. : 90 - 6927 500 - Fax : 90 - 6923 932

SVERIGE :
Svenska UNICEF-kommittén
Hantverkargaten 5 - Box 222 23 - S - 104 22 Stockholm
Tel. : (08) 692 25 00 - Fax : (08) 65 2 1520

TÜRKIYE :
UNICEF Türkiye Milli Komitesi
Abdullah Cevdet Sokak 20/10 - TR - 06680 Çankaya - Ankara
Tel. : (312) 438 17 45 / 438 00 77 - Fax : (312) 439 02 50

UNITED KINGDOM :
United Kingdom Committee for UNICEF
55, Lincolns Inn Fields - GB - London WC2A 3NB
Tel. : 171 - 405 5592 - Fax : 171-405 2332

UNITED STATES OF AMERICA :
United States Committee for UNICEF
333 East 38th Street - New York, N.Y. -10016 USA
Tel. : (212) 686-5522 - Fax : (212) 779-1679

unicef